STATES

CALIFORNIA

A MyReportLinks.com Book

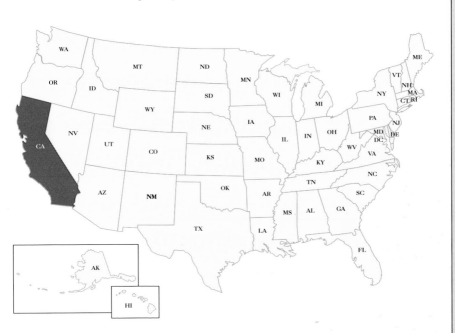

Jeff Savage

MyReportLinks.com Books

an imprint of
 Enslow Publishers, Inc.
Box 398, 40 Industrial Road
Berkeley Heights, NJ 07922
USA

MyReportLinks.com Books, an imprint of Enslow Publishers, Inc. MyReportLinks is a trademark of Enslow Publishers, Inc.

Library of Congress Cataloging-in-Publication Data

Savage, Jeff, 1961–
  California / Jeff Savage.
    p. cm. — (States)
Summary: Discusses the land and climate, economy, government, and history of the Golden State. Includes Internet links to Web sites related to California.
Includes bibliographical references and index.
  ISBN 0-7660-5113-7
  1. California—Juvenile literature. [1. California.] I. Title. II. States (Series : Berkeley Heights, N.J.)
  F861.3 .S28 2003
  979.4—dc21

                              2002153485

Printed in the United States of America

10 9 8 7 6 5 4 3 2 1

To Our Readers:
Through the purchase of this book, you and your library gain access to the Report Links that specifically back up this book.

The Publisher will provide access to the Report Links that back up this book and will keep these Report Links up to date on **www.myreportlinks.com** for three years from the book's first publication date.

We have done our best to make sure all Internet addresses in this book were active and appropriate when we went to press. However, the author and the Publisher have no control over, and assume no liability for, the material available on those Internet sites or on other Web sites they may link to.

The usage of the MyReportLinks.com Books Web site is subject to the terms and conditions stated on the Usage Policy Statement on **www.myreportlinks.com**.

In the future, a password may be required to access the Report Links that back up this book. The password is found on the bottom of page 4 of this book.

Any comments or suggestions can be sent by e-mail to comments@myreportlinks.com or to the address on the back cover.

Photo Credits: © 1998 Corbis Corporation, pp. 14, 24, 30, 33, 40; © 2001 Robesus, Inc., p. 10; © Corel Corporation, pp. 3, 13, 22; © Photodisc 1995, pp. 11, 31; Center for Steinbeck Studies, San Jose State University, p. 16; Enslow Publishers, Inc., pp. 1, 18; MyReportLinks.com Books, p. 4; Oakland Museum of California, pp. 42, 44; Richard Nixon Library & Birthplace, p. 35; Ronald Reagan Presidential Library, p. 36; The American Southwest.net, p. 20; The California Historical Society, pp. 26, 38; The Library of Congress, p. 28.

Cover Photo: Getty Images

Cover Description: The Golden Gate Bridge

Contents

MyReportLinks.com Books
Great Books, Great Links, Great for Research!

MyReportLinks.com Books present the information you need to learn about your report subject. In addition, they show you where to go on the Internet for more information. The pre-evaluated Report Links that back up this book are kept up to date on **www.myreportlinks.com**. With the purchase of a MyReportLinks.com Books title, you and your library gain access to the Report Links that specifically back up that book. The Report Links save hours of research time and link to dozens—even hundreds—of Web sites, source documents, and photos related to your report topic.

Please see "To Our Readers" on the Copyright page for important information about this book, the MyReportLinks.com Books Web site, and the Report Links that back up this book.

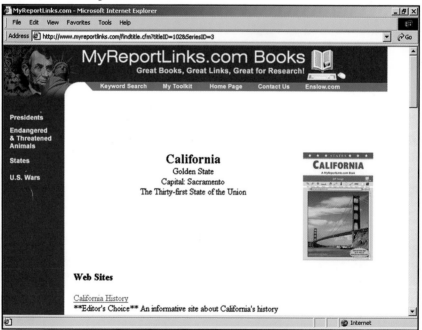

Access:

The Publisher will provide access to the Report Links that back up this book and will try to keep these Report Links up to date on our Web site for three years from the book's first publication date. Please enter **SCA5892** if asked for a password.

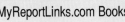
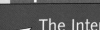

The Internet sites described below can be accessed at
http://www.myreportlinks.com

*EDITOR'S CHOICE

▶ **California History**
This comprehensive Web site features an excellent time line of the
Golden State's history. Here you can learn about California when it was
part of Mexico and read about California during the Great Depression.

Link to this Internet site from http://www.myreportlinks.com

*EDITOR'S CHOICE

▶ **Early California History: An Overview**
Explore California's early history in this Library of Congress Web site.
Here you will learn about the first people of California, Spanish
California and mission life, and much more.

Link to this Internet site from http://www.myreportlinks.com

*EDITOR'S CHOICE

▶ **U.S. Census Bureau: California**
At the U.S. Census Bureau Web site you will find statistics on
California's population, businesses, and geography.

Link to this Internet site from http://www.myreportlinks.com

*EDITOR'S CHOICE

▶ **Explore the States: California**
America's Story from America's Library, a Library of Congress Web site,
features interesting short articles about California, including stories
about logging, strawberries, and earthquakes in the state.

Link to this Internet site from http://www.myreportlinks.com

*EDITOR'S CHOICE

▶ ***World Almanac for Kids Online—California***
The *World Almanac for Kids Online* provides information about
California's land and resources, population, education, government and
politics, economy, history, and much more.

Link to this Internet site from http://www.myreportlinks.com

*EDITOR'S CHOICE

▶ **Gold Rush!**
Most everything you need to know about the California gold rush can
be found at this Web site. You can see photos, read historical accounts,
listen to portions of narratives, and even take a quiz about this pivotal
period in the state's history.

Link to this Internet site from http://www.myreportlinks.com

Report Links

The Internet sites described below can be accessed at
http://www.myreportlinks.com

▶ **California Academy of Sciences**

This interactive site has many interesting pages dedicated to the study and exploration of California's natural history. Click on "Exhibits" to explore current topics.

Link to this Internet site from http://www.myreportlinks.com

▶ **California African American Museum**

This site has images of contemporary African-American art as well as historical photos. Click on "art" and "history" to see these images.

Link to this Internet site from http://www.myreportlinks.com

▶ **California Geological Survey**

Log on to this site to learn about the geological faults in California.

Link to this Internet site from http://www.myreportlinks.com

▶ **California Guide: Death Valley National Park**

This site explores what makes Death Valley a California treasure. You can also see beautiful photos of the valley.

Link to this Internet site from http://www.myreportlinks.com

▶ **California Heritage Collection**

California's history is profiled in this site, which includes portraits of American Indians and photos of early San Francisco and California's landscape.

Link to this Internet site from http://www.myreportlinks.com

▶ **California: My Backyard**

This Sierra Club Web site is dedicated to the conservation of California's environment. Be sure to click on the John Muir Exhibition link to learn about the club's founder.

Link to this Internet site from http://www.myreportlinks.com

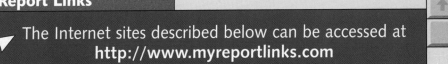

The Internet sites described below can be accessed at
http://www.myreportlinks.com

▶ **California State Railroad Museum**
Access images of trains and read about the history of railroads in
California by clicking on "Explore and Learn."

Link to this Internet site from http://www.myreportlinks.com

▶ **California State Senate**
At the California State Senate Web site you can listen to live senate
hearings, learn about current bills, and find out who California's state
senators are.

Link to this Internet site from http://www.myreportlinks.com

▶ **California Tourism**
This California Tourism Web site is a great place to find out about
California's attractions and recreational activities, its famous residents,
state icons, and more.

Link to this Internet site from http://www.myreportlinks.com

▶ **City of Los Angeles**
The City of Los Angeles Web site contains links to the museums,
libraries, and zoos of the city. Check out the Multimedia Gallery to see
photos of local art and zoo animals.

Link to this Internet site from http://www.myreportlinks.com

▶ **Computer History Museum**
The Computer History Museum is located in a part of California that
has come to be known as Silicon Valley because it is the home of so
many technology companies. This Web site explores the history of
computers and the effect of the Information Age on all of us.

Link to this Internet site from http://www.myreportlinks.com

▶ **50 States: California**
In this site, find out when California became a state; what the state
flag, bird, and motto are; and other interesting facts about the
Golden State.

Link to this Internet site from http://www.myreportlinks.com

 The Internet sites described below can be accessed at
http://www.myreportlinks.com

▶ **La Brea Tar Pits**
See photos of Ice Age fossils discovered at the La Brea Tar Pits in Los Angeles.

Link to this Internet site from http://www.myreportlinks.com

▶ **LearnCalifornia**
This is an electronic resource for students and others who are interested in California history. Click on the Students link to find out about California during the Great Depression, the Great San Francisco Earthquake, and more.

Link to this Internet site from http://www.myreportlinks.com

▶ **Methuselah Tree**
This fascinating site explores the majestic wonder of ancient bristlecone pines—the world's oldest trees—in California's White Mountains. Click on "Explore the Methuselah Grove" to get a panoramic view.

Link to this Internet site from http://www.myreportlinks.com

▶ **Official California Legislative Information**
At the Official California Legislative Information Web site you can find information about bills, laws, and the California legislature.

Link to this Internet site from http://www.myreportlinks.com

▶ **Richard M. Nixon**
Read about the life and political career of President Richard Nixon, who was born in California in 1913.

Link to this Internet site from http://www.myreportlinks.com

▶ **Ronald Reagan**
This Web site contains facts about the life and political career of Ronald Reagan, who served two terms as California's governor before being elected president of the United States.

Link to this Internet site from http://www.myreportlinks.com

Report Links

The Internet sites described below can be accessed at
http://www.myreportlinks.com

▶ **San Diego Zoo**

This famous zoo's Web site features fun facts and great photos of some
of the animals to be found at the San Diego Zoo. Make sure to click on
"kid territory" to read animal profiles, learn about science experiments,
and find out how to make zoo crafts.

Link to this Internet site from http://www.myreportlinks.com

▶ **San Francisco**

The San Francisco Web site contains fun facts, statistics, photos,
history, and current information about the City by the Bay.

Link to this Internet site from http://www.myreportlinks.com

▶ **San Francisco Chinatown**

San Francsico's Chinatown is a vibrant community with a long and
interesting history. This Web site explores that history and even shows
visitors how to hold chopsticks properly.

Link to this Internet site from http://www.myreportlinks.com

▶ **San Francisco Museum**

The Great Fire and Earthquake of 1906 nearly destroyed San Francisco.
This site features newspaper transcripts from that time as well as
eyewitness accounts of the events that rocked the city.

Link to this Internet site from http://www.myreportlinks.com

▶ **Welcome to California**

Learn about California's economy, educational centers, tourism, history,
and culture. This Welcome to California Web site is a great place to
start learning about the Golden State.

Link to this Internet site from http://www.myreportlinks.com

▶ **Yosemite National Park**

At this site you'll learn about one of the most famous national parks in
the United States: Yosemite, which is found in California's Sierra
Nevada. Learn about its history, current weather conditions, bear
activity, and more.

Link to this Internet site from http://www.myreportlinks.com

▷ **Capital**
Sacramento

▷ **Population**
33,871,648*

▷ **Gained Statehood**
September 9, 1850

▷ **Bird**
California valley quail

▷ **Tree**
California redwood

▷ **Flower**
Golden poppy

▷ **Animal**
California grizzly bear

▷ **Fish**
California golden trout

▷ **Insect**
California dogface butterfly

▷ **Marine Mammal**
California gray whale

▷ **Song**
"I Love You, California," music
by A. F. Frankenstein and lyrics
by F. B. Silverwood

▷ **Motto**
Eureka
(Greek for "I have found it!")

▷ **Flag**
A white background featuring a
grizzly bear and the inscription
"California Republic" below the
bear, a red star in the upper-left
corner, and a red border at the
bottom.

▷ **Nickname**
The Golden State

▷ **Fossil**
Saber-toothed cat

▷ **Reptile**
Desert tortoise

Population reflects the 2000 census.

The State of California

California is a state that seems to have everything. The landscape ranges from sandy beaches and white-hot deserts to snow-capped mountains and redwood forests. There are more people in California than in any other state, and they represent nearly every ethnic group in the world. California has more computer technicians, farmers, surfers, and movie stars than any other state. It is the leading state in mining, agriculture, and manufactured goods. In fact, California produces so much that if it were a separate country, it would rank fifth in the world in gross national product.

▲ Mount Shasta in northern California's Cascade range is the second highest volcano in the United States.

The Promised Land

For most of its history, California has been considered the land of opportunity, and people have been pouring into California for more than a century. They come north from Mexico, sail in from the Pacific Ocean to the west, and drive across state lines from other states to the east and north. Nearly 1 million new residents arrive each year. With a population of 34.5 million, nearly one out of every eight Americans lives in California.[1]

Almost 500 years ago, the American Indians who lived in the area were surprised to learn of the arrival of explorers from Spain and England. Settlers from Spain and New Spain (Mexico) established missions in California in the mid-1700s. They were followed by settlers from Russia and elsewhere. The discovery of gold at Sutter's Mill in the foothills east of Sacramento in 1848 drew thousands to that region by 1849, especially from the New England states, New York, and Pennsylvania. California became a state a year later, and soon hordes of people from the Midwest and elsewhere were headed to California on horse-drawn wagon trains, seeking wealth and a better way of life. Rich farmland was a special attraction at that time. By the twentieth century, jobs in commerce and industry were luring many more people.

Modern California is as ethnically diverse as the land itself. Latinos and people of African and Asian ancestry make up about half the state's population. More people of Mexican ancestry live in Los Angeles, California's largest city, than any other area in the world outside Mexico. A rising tide of undocumented Mexican workers, estimated to be in the millions, is not counted in the state's official statistics. Among the largest Chinese communities outside China itself is Chinatown in San Francisco, with a population of more than 30,000. Nearly a quarter million American Indians live in California.

A Golden State

With so many people in California, you might think the state is filled to capacity, but there is still plenty of room for growth. With four of the nation's largest cities in California, there is certainly urban sprawl. But with a land area of 155,973 square miles, California is the third-largest state in area after Alaska and Texas, and it is still home to vast stretches of wilderness and undeveloped land.[2]

California features eighteen national forests and eight national parks. These forests and parks occupy more than one fourth of the total land area of the state. The state's scenic beauty prompts some visitors to return home, pack their belongings, and move to the Golden State for good.

▲ This traditional Mexican plaza is not in Mexico but on Olvera Street in Los Angeles, the oldest part of the City of Angels.

California is known for dramatic natural wonders that include redwood groves, geysers, and volcanic cones. The most popular park is Yosemite National Park, in the heart of the Sierra Nevada. Yosemite features granite domes, sheer cliffs, and cascading waterfalls. Naturalist, writer, and conservationist John Muir is credited with leading the drive to have Congress designate Yosemite as a national park in 1890. Muir, known as the "father of our national parks," later founded a conservation group called the Sierra Club.

Among the most popular national monuments in California is Death Valley, a desolate area in the Mojave

▲ Yosemite National Park's majestic peaks, beautiful waterfalls, and ancient forests in California's Sierra Nevada have been preserved as a wilderness area since 1890.

Desert in the southern part of the state. At 282 feet below sea level, Badwater in Death Valley is the lowest point in the continental United States. The sun scorches the earth there by day, and then as it sets each evening, it transforms the ground and sky into brilliant colors and hues. California is also the site of the highest point outside of Alaska in the continental United States: Mount Whitney, whose summit is 14,495 feet above sea level—and only an hour's drive from Death Valley. With such a diverse landscape, it is no wonder that California often records both the highest and lowest temperatures in the continental United States in the same day.

▶ California Writers

California's unique way of life has inspired many writers who were either born there or lived much of their life in the state. The list reads like a who's who of famous writers.

Although born in Missouri, Mark Twain lived in San Francisco and the Sierra Nevada, and he first gained fame for his short story "The Celebrated Jumping Frog of Calaveras County" and his novel *Roughing It*. His most popular works were *Tom Sawyer* and *The Adventures of Huckleberry Finn*. Jack London, who was born in San Francisco, wrote *Call of the Wild* and other adventure stories. John Steinbeck, who was born in Salinas, won a Pulitzer Prize for *The Grapes of Wrath*, the story of poor tenant farmers in Oklahoma who move to California during the dust bowl of the 1930s. Steinbeck was also awarded the 1962 Nobel Prize in literature. Several of his novels have been made into movies. Likewise, William Saroyan, who was born in Fresno, won a Pulitzer Prize for his play *The Time of Your Life*. Robert Frost, born in San Francisco, was one of America's leading twentieth-century

John Steinbeck, considered one of America's greatest writers, was born in Salinas, California, in 1902. He is seen here receiving the 1962 Nobel Prize in literature.

poets and a four-time winner of the Pulitzer Prize. San Franciscan Dashiell Hammett wrote *The Maltese Falcon, The Thin Man,* and other detective stories. Raymond Chandler of Los Angeles created the popular private investigator Philip Marlowe. Jack Kerouac, who lived in San Francisco and Berkeley, wrote about the Beat generation of the 1950s in his novel *On the Road.* Theodore Geisel, better known as Dr. Seuss, lived in La Jolla and wrote wonderful children's books, including *The Cat in the Hat.* Charles Schultz, who lived in Santa Rosa, is the creator of the cartoon characters Charlie Brown, Snoopy, and the rest of the cast of *Peanuts.* Current novelists include Alice Walker, the author of *The Color Purple,* who lives in Mendocino, and Amy Tan, author of *The Joy Luck Club,* who was born in Oakland.

Land and Climate

California shares its border with three states, one country, and one ocean. To the north is Oregon, to the east is Nevada, and to the southeast is Arizona. The state lines with Oregon and Nevada are primarily straight. The border with Arizona is jagged and formed by the Colorado River. The southern border with Mexico is straight. To the west is the Pacific Ocean. The coastline is 840 miles long, the third-longest seacoast after Alaska and Florida.

▶ A Varied Climate

On New Year's Day, many Americans watch the Tournament of Roses Parade and then the Rose Bowl football game on television, broadcast from Pasadena in sunny southern California. They see the sunny skies and warm weather and dream of escaping harsh winter climes. But while it may be sunny and warm in Pasadena, it might be raining, hailing, or snowing elsewhere in the state. The weather in California is as varied as the landscape. And unlike the weather in much of the rest of the nation, the weather in California is quite predictable.

Along the narrow coastline in southern California, the climate is mild year-round, with little precipitation. San Diego, near the southern end of the state, has an average temperature of 61°F and receives an average of 10.3 inches of rain per year. The farther north one travels, the more it rains and the colder it gets. San Francisco, just above the halfway point of the state, averages 56°F and 22 inches of rain annually. Fog also develops along the coast, particularly in the northern region. San Francisco is famous for its fog, or condensed air, which forms as the ocean breeze meets the coastal current.

The southern interior of the state is hot and dry. Some places receive no measurable rain all year. There is so little humidity in the Colorado and Mojave Deserts that temperatures nearing 100°F are tolerable. But it can get much hotter. In 1913, in Death Valley, the temperature hit

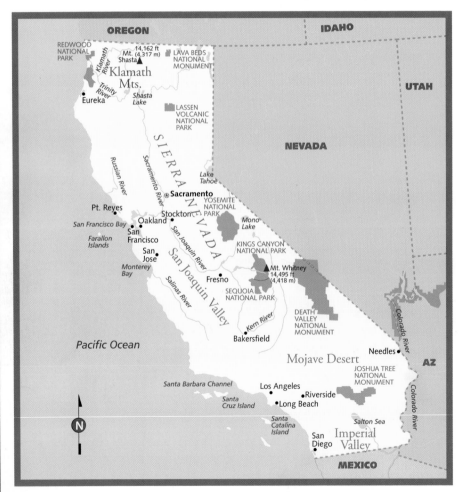

▲ A map of California.

134°F degrees, the hottest temperature ever recorded in North America.[1] The desert winds sometimes blow across the Santa Ana Mountains into the cities along the coast. These are called Santa Ana winds, and they lift coastal temperatures into the 90s. Farther north, the inland central valleys are hot and dry in the summer and cold and damp in the winter. In the colder months, this area develops tule fog, which rises up from the ground and can reduce visibility to mere feet. Motorists must pull to the side of the road and sometimes wait hours until the fog clears.

Along much of the eastern portion of the state is the mountain range known as the Sierra Nevada, 50 to 80 miles wide and more than 400 miles long. *Sierra Nevada* is Spanish for "snowy range," which is an appropriate name: Heavy snowfall packs the range at a rate of 445 inches per year, most of it falling from December to March. The snowfall is reliable and an important source of water. The 1960 Olympic Winter Games were held at Squaw Valley near Lake Tahoe, where there is always plenty of snow in the winter, and the temperature once dropped to −45°F, the lowest temperature ever recorded in the state.

▷ Shifting Plates

California's landscape was formed millions of years ago by shifting tectonic plates, which are sections of the earth's crust. The Pacific Plate, to the west, slipped underneath the North American Plate, and its edge pushed up and through, forming mountain ranges. The pressure between the plates caused so much heat that active volcanoes formed. (The last volcano to erupt in California was Mount Lassen in 1921.) The southeastern portion of the state stretched and sank below sea level and was covered by the ocean. Two groups of islands were formed off the coast.

The Santa Barbara Islands (also called the Channel Islands) are northwest of Los Angeles, and the Farallon Islands are west of San Francisco. During the last Ice Age, glaciers carved paths on the eastern side of the state through mountains and hills, forming narrow valleys, river streams, and sheer granite cliffs.

Lakes and Rivers

California has about eight thousand lakes, but many are actually reservoirs that have been created by dams. Most lakes are in the northern two thirds of the state. The southern section is nearly dry. Lake Tahoe is the largest freshwater

California Guide - Pictures of Death Valley National Park - Microsoft Internet Explorer

File   Edit   View   Favorites   Tools   Help   Links »

Address http://www.americansouthwest.net/california/death_valley/desolation2_1.html

View from the top of Desolation Canyon - over the north end of Artist's Drive and the Death Valley salt flats

Internet

Death Valley, whose stark landscape is pictured, is the site of the lowest point in the continental United States. It is also where the highest temperature on record in North America was recorded.

lake, but its eastern half sits across the border in Nevada. There is enough water in Lake Tahoe to cover the entire state in fourteen inches of water. The largest freshwater lake entirely within the state is Clear Lake, north of the Napa Valley. The Salton Sea, in the southern desert of the Imperial Valley, is actually larger. It was an ancient dry bed until 1905 when the Colorado River flooded and spilled into it. Over the years, the water has become salty and undrinkable. California's largest rivers are the Sacramento and San Joaquin Rivers, which move through the Central Valley. Many of the other large rivers in the state flow into one of these two. The Sacramento flows south, and the San Joaquin flows north, and they converge to form a delta at San Francisco Bay.

▶ "From the Redwood Forests"

Forestlands cover more than 40 percent of California. The coastal redwoods in the northwestern area of the state are the tallest trees on earth. Some redwoods stand as tall as 370 feet and live for more than two thousand years. The giant sequoia trees of the Sierra Nevada live even longer, an average of 3,200 years. The world's largest tree, a sequoia nicknamed the General Sherman tree, grows in the high Sierra. It is not as tall as some redwoods, but its weight is calculated at 6,167 tons, which is the same as 41 blue whales or 740 full-grown elephants. The most common trees in California are firs and pines. There are several varieties of pines, including Torrey, Jeffrey, sugar, ponderosa, and bristlecone. A bristlecone pine named Methuselah in the eastern Inyo National Forest is believed to be, at 4,700 years old, the oldest living tree on earth.[2] Other common trees are black oak and aspen in the mountains, eucalyptus throughout the state, and palm trees in the south. Much of

▲ *A view of Mount Lassen from Manzanita Lake, Lassen Volcanic National Park.*

the undeveloped land in the south is covered with thorny chaparral shrubs a few feet tall. In the north, the golden grasses that cover the hillsides in summer and fall give California its nickname, the Golden State.

▷ Animals of the Wild and Human Variety

California's unique vegetation supports four hundred species of mammals and six hundred types of birds. Squirrels, chipmunks, and coyotes are everywhere. Lizards, rattlesnakes, jackrabbits, desert tortoises, horned toads, kangaroo rats, and pronghorn antelope can all be found in California's deserts. Among the woodland and forest animals found in the state are deer, foxes, bobcats, weasels, elk, and black bears. At higher elevations in the mountains are cougars, wolverines, and mountain lions. Common birds include juncos, California jays, bluebirds, ravens, eagles, Valley quail, mourning doves, wood ducks, and geese. There is a widespread effort to save the nearly extinct California condor. Lakes and streams teem with trout and salmon. Gray whales can be seen in the waters off California's Pacific coast.

California's vast expanses are sparsely populated. Nine out of every ten people live in urban centers. These densely populated areas are mainly along the coast. In the south-land, a sprawling urban area marked by houses and pavement has developed from San Diego over 100 miles northward to Los Angeles and beyond, then eastward 30 miles across the great Inland Empire. In northern California, another megalopolis has been built around San Francisco Bay, which includes the cities of San Francisco, Oakland, and San Jose. The largest inland urban areas are Sacramento and Fresno.

▷ Earthquake!

California has been the site of some of the most devastating earthquakes in the United States. Earthquakes are caused when tectonic plates, or fractures in the earth's crust, shift and grind against one another. The place where these plates meet is called a fault. There are numerous faults in California. The largest fault is the San Andreas Fault, which enters northern California from the Pacific Ocean and runs southward into southern California.

Earthquakes happen in California every day. The movement is so subtle, however, that they are hardly ever felt. On rare occasions, though, the ground shifts enough

▲ *Some of the tallest and oldest trees in the world are found in the Sequoia National Forest. Giant sequoia trees may reach heights in excess of 300 feet.*

to cause a jolt felt by those nearby. In the worst cases, the ground shakes so violently that structures collapse. The last major earthquake occurred in 1994 in an urban area of southern California. Two years earlier, a larger quake took place in a southern California mountain area. And in 1989, the San Francisco Bay Area was rocked by a severe quake.

Economy

California is blessed with an abundance of natural resources. Most of the state receives sufficient sunshine and rain for growing crops and has fertile soil rich in minerals. California is easily the nation's leading agricultural state, producing more than half of all the nuts, fruits, and vegetables sold in the United States.[1] California also leads the nation in mining, fishing, manufactured goods, and many other areas of production.

▶ Cultivating the Earth

California's Central Valley stretches over three hundred miles north to south and is as wide as eighty miles east to west. This enormous fertile valley produces crops of every imaginable color and shape. California is the country's top producer of avocados, potatoes, asparagus, carrots, celery, melons, olives, tomatoes, onions, apricots, almonds, walnuts, pistachios, nectarines, cantaloupes, kiwifruit, plums, peaches, and pears. The Salinas Valley nearer the coast of Monterey leads the nation in the production of lettuce, broccoli, cauliflower, artichokes, and spinach. Other areas specialize in growing a single crop. Vineyards in the Napa Valley above San Francisco Bay produce grapes for some of the finest wines in the world. Farms around Gilroy, south of the Bay Area, produce garlic. California is also the leading dairy state in the nation. Thanks to more than one million dairy cows, milk and cream are the state's top farm products.

Water for the Valley

None of this production would be possible without water, and the rivers that flow through the Central Valley do not provide nearly enough water. Almost 40 percent of California's water reserves are in the northwestern part of the state, where only 2 percent of the people live. Since the early 1900s, engineers working for the state government have managed to design and build large irrigation systems to move water from one area to another. California has an estimated 8,000 lakes, but most of them are man-made

http://www.californiahistory.net/8images/hetch2_lrg.jpg - Microsoft Internet Explorer

File   Edit   View   Favorites   Tools   Help   Links »

Address http://www.californiahistory.net/8images/hetch2_lrg.jpg

8781. 6,7,23 Hetch Hetchy Reservoir

Done   Internet

The Hetch Hetchy Reservoir, which was created by a dam built across the Tuolumne River, provides nearly 85 percent of San Francisco's water supply. The reservoir was built over the objections of many conservationists, including John Muir, who died soon after Congress approved the project in 1913.

reservoirs. Among the largest are Lakes Shasta, Berryessa, Folsom, Arrowhead, and Cachuma. Water is drawn from these lakes and many others to the fields and elsewhere. Two key structures for valley irrigation are Shasta Dam and Friant Dam. Here water is stored and then carried through aqueducts. Similar designs on a larger scale, such as Hoover Dam and Parker Dam on the Colorado River near Las Vegas, Nevada, provide water to Los Angeles, and the Hetch Hetchy Reservoir on the Tuolumne River carries water to San Francisco.

▷ Wealth From the Land and Seas

Almost all of California's land is rich in minerals. The best known, of course, is gold, which was discovered in the mid-nineteenth century and scooped from the ground at a furious rate by thousands of miners. Geologists estimate that 70 percent of the gold is still in California's Gold Country, and California remains a leading gold-producing state. The most valuable mineral to the state today is "black gold," otherwise known as petroleum, or oil. There are vast pools of petroleum beneath the soil of the southern Central Valley and along the coastline. California has more than 40,000 working oil wells, ranking it near the top among state production. Natural gas is another important energy source for the state, and it is found throughout the Central Valley. Petroleum and natural gas account for nearly three fourths of the state's mining production. California is also the only state with borax deposits. This mineral is used to make common kitchen cleansers. Other minerals mined from California's rich soil include silver, copper, asbestos, tungsten, zinc, mercury, magnesium, pumice, gypsum, sand, and gravel.

Pictured are loggers in the process of falling an old-growth redwood in northern California. The timber industry is an important part of California's economy.

California employs a large timber industry, second only to Oregon. Lumber is used to build houses and make furniture and paper products as well as for firewood. Redwoods are harvested from the Coast Ranges, and pines and firs are logged from the Sierra.

California is among the top-five states in the amount of seafood produced. Its fresh seafood is pulled from the coastal waters and delivered everywhere. Among the most frequent catches are yellowfin and albacore tuna, anchovies, mackerel, salmon, and shellfish such as abalone and crab.

Manufacturing

More than 2 million people work in factories in California, producing an array of products from the spacecraft for the nation's space program to chips and circuitry used in personal computers. Fighter planes and guided missiles are developed and tested at military bases and weapons centers in the state. More commercial aircraft are built in California than in any other state, and major automobile plants can be found in California's urban centers. Scientific instruments and electronic components are designed and crafted by high-tech industries mostly in an area at the southern end of San Francisco Bay known as Silicon Valley. It is so named because computer chips are made of a material called silicon. This area is the birthplace of the personal computer industry.

California's Brain Trust

California is home to many laboratories that conduct research and test new products. Most are located near universities to take advantage of the brainpower of scientists and engineers from those universities. California is a leader in modern science and engineering largely because of its excellent system of higher education. The University of California system opened in 1868, and several of its campuses, particularly UC Berkeley and UC San Diego, rank among the nation's top centers for research. Stanford University in the Bay Area is also among the finest centers of higher learning in the nation.

Of course, the motion-picture industry, which had its beginnings in the Golden State, is still extremely important to California's economy. Director D. W. Griffith started it all with the movie *The Birth of a Nation* in 1915, and

▲ *The famous Hollywood sign was erected as a temporary advertisement by a real-estate developer in 1923. The sign was designated a Los Angeles Cultural Historic Landmark in 1973, ensuring that it will remain an icon for years to come.*

Hollywood, a community within the city of Los Angeles, has become synonymous with filmmaking and the television industry ever since. Although many films and television series are now shot "on location"—in cities throughout the world—Hollywood is still the symbolic capital of the film and television industries in the United States, and as such, attracts many tourists.

▷ Getting There

Los Angeles is the major business center of the western United States, with the Bay Area ranking second. To accommodate heavy automobile traffic in and around these areas, an intricate road system has been built that features freeways with overpasses, underpasses, and cloverleafs. Bridges are among many state landmarks, but they also serve to shuttle hundreds of thousands of vehicles daily. The multileveled San Francisco-Oakland Bay Bridge that spans the bay between the two cities is 8.4 miles in length (including approaches and a toll plaza), one of the longest in the world. With millions of cars on the road each day, the skies over some areas of the state sometimes have a grayish-brown haze. This is called smog, a combination of the words "smoke" and "fog."

The Tourism Industry

With all California has to offer, it is little wonder that the state teems with tourists. San Francisco tops travel polls as the number-one city in the world, welcoming more than 17 million tourists each year. Visitors come to see such sites as the Golden Gate Bridge, which marks the entrance to the bay from the Pacific Ocean. The bridge is painted regularly with 5,000 gallons of orange paint. Among the attractions of San Francisco are windy Lombard Street, called the "crookedest street in the world"; Fisherman's Wharf, which features seafood vendors and restaurants;

San Francisco's famed cable cars have been transporting San Franciscans up and down the hilly city's streets since 1873.

numerous museums and parks; and the famed cable cars. Tourists can take a ferry across the bay to places such as Alcatraz, the island prison that held such dangerous criminals as Al Capone and "Machine Gun" Kelly before it closed in 1963. Just north of San Francisco is the wine country of Napa and Sonoma, where travelers sip wines and enjoy gourmet meals or take hot-air balloon rides. To the east near Sacramento is Sutter's Fort and Sutter's Mill, where gold was first discovered in California. South from there is world-renowned Yosemite National Park. Back along the coast near the famous Pebble Beach golf course is the Monterey Bay Aquarium, one of the largest aquariums in the world, which features a two-story otter exhibit and a three-story kelp forest. Farther south near San Luis Obispo is Hearst Castle, the elaborate estate of publisher and tycoon William Randolph Hearst, whose life was depicted in the award-winning movie *Citizen Kane*.

Tourists travel to the southern end of the state to visit Universal Studios Hollywood to see how movies are made or watch a television show being filmed. Others spend money at expensive shops in nearby Beverly Hills. Disneyland is a favorite attraction, drawing 14 million visitors each year. It features many rides and "lands" such as Fantasyland and Tomorrowland, and is known as "The Happiest Place on Earth." Farther south in San Diego is Sea World, a marine zoological park featuring killer whales, dolphins, sea lions, and otters, and the world-famous San Diego Zoo. Traveling east, the beauty of the Joshua Tree National Monument and the Anza-Borrego Desert State Park are to be found. For the tourist and resident alike, there are plenty of recreational facilities in California, including ski slopes, beaches, hiking trails, and world-famous golf courses.

Government

Even before California was granted statehood, it had a constitution. That constitution was adopted in 1849 in Monterey, the state's first capital, one year before the territory became the thirty-first state in the Union.[1] The present constitution was adopted in 1879. It has been amended more than three hundred times since then.

For the framework of their state government, Californians used the United States Constitution as a guide. The state constitution divides the power between three branches of government: the executive, the legislative, and the judicial. The governor, elected to a four-year term, oversees the executive branch. Other key state officials include the lieutenant governor, who serves if the governor cannot; the secretary of state, who maintains public records; the attorney general, who acts as the chief attorney for the state; and the treasurer,

California's capitol building, ▶ in Sacramento. Constructed in 1874, the capitol features a dome similar to that of the United States Capitol.

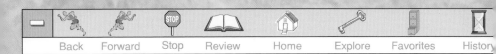
who helps manage the state's money. These officials are also elected to four-year terms, and none may serve more than two terms.

The Legislature

The California legislature is the law-making branch of state government. It consists of a senate of forty members and an assembly of eighty members. Senators are elected to four-year terms and may serve no more than two terms. Assembly members, called representatives, are elected to two-year terms and may serve up to three terms. For a proposal to become law, it must pass both houses of the legislature by a majority vote and then be signed by the governor. If the governor vetoes the proposal, or refuses to sign it, the proposal returns to the legislature. The proposal can still become law if both houses then pass it by at least a two-thirds majority, known as an override.

California Courts

California's judicial branch has three levels of trial courts—municipal, justice, and superior. The state has fifty-eight counties, and each county has one superior court. Trial-court rulings may be challenged at one of five district appeals courts in the state. Another challenge takes the case to the state supreme court. A final appeal can be taken to the U.S. Supreme Court.

The Power of the People

During the California gold rush days, when gold strikes prompted looting and other crooked deeds, Californians swiftly took matters into their own hands. They formed vigilante groups to capture crooks and punish them. The worst felons were sentenced to death by hanging. The town of Placerville, in the foothills east of Sacramento, is still known as "Hangtown." Californians prefer a more civilized form of government these days, but they have always insisted on having their own voice, and they designed their constitution with this in mind.

California citizens can pass laws directly. Two direct-participation laws give ordinary citizens that ability. The first is through the process of an "initiative." At least 5 percent of eligible voters must sign a petition in favor of a measure for it to be put on the ballot for the next general election. If the voters approve the measure by a simple majority, the measure becomes law. The second means is through the power of "referendum." If 5 percent of eligible voters sign a petition that challenges a law passed by the legislature, that law may be put on the ballot. The law will not go into effect unless a majority of citizens vote in favor of it.

▶ Noteworthy Politicians

Just as California is the nation's leader in economic production, it has also produced many famous politicians, including two U.S. presidents, Richard

▶ *Richard Nixon, the thirty-seventh president of the United States, was born in Yorba Linda, California, and grew up there and in Whittier.*

Nixon and Ronald Reagan. Nixon was born in Yorba Linda, in southern California. He served as a congressman and as vice president under President Dwight Eisenhower before running for president in 1960. In that election, Nixon was narrowly defeated by John F. Kennedy, but he ran again eight years later and became the thirty-seventh president. He was reelected in 1972, but he was forced to resign two years later over the Watergate scandal. Nixon was a Republican, and so, too, was Ronald Reagan.

Reagan, born in Illinois, was a sports broadcaster and then a Hollywood actor before entering politics. His acting skills and smooth style helped him present his ideas to people, and they responded enthusiastically. Reagan was elected governor of California in 1966 and again in 1970. He won the presidency in 1980 and again in 1984.

Another popular California governor was Earl Warren, who became chief justice of the United States. Warren was born in Los Angeles, but he began his political career as district attorney of Alameda County in the Bay Area. He was elected California's governor in 1942 and was

Although he was not born in California, Ronald Reagan has spent much of his adult life there. The Reagans continue to live at their beloved Rancho del Cielo (the "ranch in the sky") in the Santa Ynez Mountains.

reelected twice, serving a total of ten years before term limits were established. In 1953, President Eisenhower appointed Warren chief justice of the United States—the highest judicial position in the land. Warren's term as chief justice was noteworthy for the 1954 Supreme Court ruling that outlawed segregation in public schools. Ten years later, Warren was appointed chairman of a committee that investigated the assassination of President John F. Kennedy.

Edmund G. "Pat" Brown served as California's governor from 1959 to 1967, between Warren and Reagan. He was a liberal Democrat who improved welfare programs for the poor. His son, Edmund G. "Jerry" Brown, became governor after Reagan. Jerry Brown's politics were even more liberal than his father's, and he preferred living in a small apartment in Sacramento instead of taking up residence in the governor's mansion. Jerry Brown later made an unsuccessful bid for the U.S. presidency and then became the mayor of Oakland. Across the bay, in San Francisco, Willie Brown is another mayor with a unique style. Flamboyant, even controversial, his undeniable charm makes him popular. Before Willie Brown became mayor, the office was held by Dianne Feinstein, the first woman elected mayor of San Francisco, in 1988. Four years later, Feinstein became the state's first woman elected U.S. senator. A Democrat, Feinstein has ascended the ranks, taking seats on the Senate's Foreign Relations, Judiciary, and Rules Committees. As Feinstein was being elected to Congress in 1992, so, too, was Barbara Boxer. Together they became the first pair of women to be elected to the Senate from the same state in the same year. Before being elected to the Senate, Boxer served in the House of Representatives for ten years. She was reelected senator in 1998 for a second six-year term and continues to champion education and women's causes.

History

In June 1542, Juan Rodríguez Cabrillo, a Portuguese explorer working for Spain, set sail from New Spain (Mexico) in search of a fantasy "island called California." The Spanish had read about this mythical paradise of gold in a novel written more than thirty years earlier. Cabrillo sailed north, and on September 28, 1542, he entered San Diego Bay. He was the first European to sight what is now

▲ This early-nineteenth-century painting by a French artist depicts the diverse American Indian culture that once existed in California.

California. Cabrillo died during the voyage, but his crew sailed on as far north as Cape Mendocino. They apparently missed the wide port into San Francisco Bay, later known as the Golden Gate. It was discovered in 1579 by Sir Francis Drake of England, who claimed the land for Queen Elizabeth I. These and other explorers were latecomers to a land that had been inhabited long before.

As many as 15,000 years earlier, Asian people had entered the North American continent from Siberia across a land bridge that has since become submerged beneath the ocean. These people spread across the land in groups. The Hupa people lived in northwestern California. The Maidu lived in the central section. The Quechan lived in the south. Other American Indian groups included the Ohlone, Miwok, Yokut, Paiute, Pomo, Modoc, and Cahuilla. These groups survived by fishing and hunting and gathering berries and nuts.

▶ The Arrival of Missions and Settlers

The Spanish were intent on extending their empire northward from New Spain. Franciscan friars wished to spread the word of Christianity. Together they traveled by both land and sea into California to build missions, presidios (military forts), and pueblos (agricultural towns). A Catholic priest, Father Junípero Serra, and two officials of New Spain, José de Gálvez and Gaspar de Portolá, led the way. In 1769, Serra opened his first mission, San Diego de Alcala, with a presidio nearby.[1] Monterey's presidio opened the following year. By 1823, twenty-one missions spread from San Diego to Sonoma on what became known as *El Camino Real*, Spanish for "the Royal Road." Each mission was about one day's walk from the next. Missionaries attempted to convert the American Indians to Christianity

▲ *San Diego de Alcala, opened in 1769 by Father Junípero Serra, was the first mission church in California. The church continues to operate as a parish church of the Diocese of San Diego.*

but had little success. Angered by the Spanish, normally peaceful tribes swept down upon the missions and presidios to fight.

After Mexico gained its freedom from Spain in 1821, it declared the mission churches powerless and took control of the land in California. Pueblo lands were then given away to Mexican ranchers, farmers, and soldiers who called themselves "Californios." The Californios established large estates called ranchos on which cattle were raised. Until the 1840s, most of the colonization of California was Mexican.

In 1826, fur trapper Jedediah Smith led an expedition from the Salt Lake valley across the Mojave Desert into southern California. He was the first white man to cross the Sierra Nevada and the first to cross the Great Salt Lake

Desert. His journey and that of John Augustus Sutter, who in 1839 established his own "kingdom" on land near Sacramento, prompted a wave of American settlers to move west by the 1840s. As more American settlers poured in, the Californios grew nervous.

Manifest Destiny and War With Mexico

Texas was another territory that belonged to Mexico at the time. But in 1836, Texas gained its independence from Mexico after a bloody revolutionary war. At news of this, Americans in California believed more than ever in "manifest destiny"—the belief that America was destined to expand its territory to the Pacific Ocean. In 1845 the Californios drove out the last Mexican governor of California. In 1846, Army officer John C. Frémont and other settlers proclaimed a republic at Sonoma and raised their own flag, which depicted a bear, in defiance of Mexican offi-cials. In July 1846, during the Mexican-American War, a U.S. naval force under Commodore John D. Sloat sailed into San Francisco Bay and declared California a territory of the United States. The boundary dispute soon ended in a U.S. victory, and on February 2, 1848, with the Treaty of Guadalupe Hidalgo, Mexico was forced to give up about half of its territory in America, from Texas to the Pacific Ocean. That territory included California.

The Forty-Niners: Gold Fever

Nine days before the peace treaty between the United States and Mexico was signed, making California a United States territory, gold was discovered at Sutter's Mill in the foothills east of Sacramento. James Marshall was building a sawmill on the American River for his boss, John Sutter, when he found several yellow nuggets in the water. The

The Art of the Gold Rush - Portrait of General John A. Sutter - Microsoft Internet Explorer

File   Edit   View   Favorites   Tools   Help   Links »

Address   http://www.museumca.org/goldrush/art-gesutter.html

GOLD
FEVER!

SILVER
& GOLD

NATIVES &
IMMIGRANTS

Portrait of General John A. Sutter

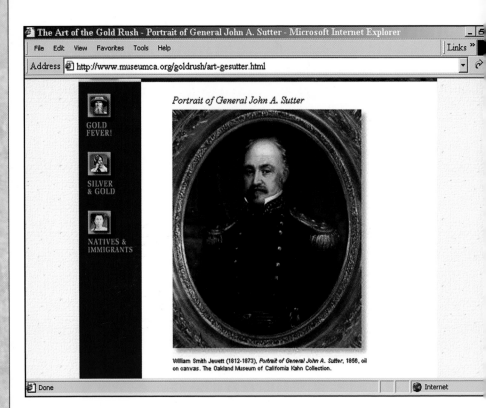

William Smith Jewett (1812-1873), *Portrait of General John A. Sutter*, 1856, oil
on canvas. The Oakland Museum of California Kahn Collection.

Done   Internet

*John Augustus Sutter was an early settler and landowner in California.
It was at his mill on the American River outside Sacramento that gold
was discovered in 1848, leading to the California gold rush.*

discovery of gold in California triggered one of the biggest migrations in the history of the world. Within a few months, thousands of people from San Francisco and elsewhere along the coast had streamed into the Central Valley and foothills to pan for gold.

By late summer, word spread to the rest of the country. In December 1848, President James Polk announced that gold was in California for the taking, and "gold fever" swept the nation. By February 1849, 130 ships had sailed from the East Coast for California. A year later, the number of ships had risen to 17,000. Thousands more sailed in

from Europe and Asia. Those who traveled to California to mine gold became known as the forty-niners, marking the year of the mass migration.

Mining camps made of tents and log cabins were set up along the foothills of the Sierra. The area became known as the Mother Lode Country. Living conditions were harsh. Some prospectors struck it rich, but most miners found nothing but heartache. Some returned home, but many stayed to make a new life as farmers and merchants.

Drive Toward Statehood

The huge increase in the territory's population brought with it a need for government, and Californians pressed Congress in 1849 for statehood. On September 9, 1850, California was admitted to the Union as a free state (one where slavery was not permitted) through the terms of the Compromise of 1850. San Jose, Monterey, Vallejo, and Benicia each served as the state capital until 1854, when Sacramento was designated the state capital.

In the 1850s and 1860s, California became connected with the rest of the country, first by overland mail via the Pony Express, next by telegraph, and finally, by the construction of railroads, built mostly by Chinese laborers.

The Asian Presence in California

The issue of Asian immigration has been a complicated one in California's history. In the 1860s, when Chinese laborers were recruited to build the railroads, immigration from China was unrestricted. But when the state's economy went into a slump, white settlers resented the lower-paid Chinese laborers, and their resentment led to the passage in 1881 of federal laws that restricted Chinese immigration. Later, as Japanese farmers began to buy valuable

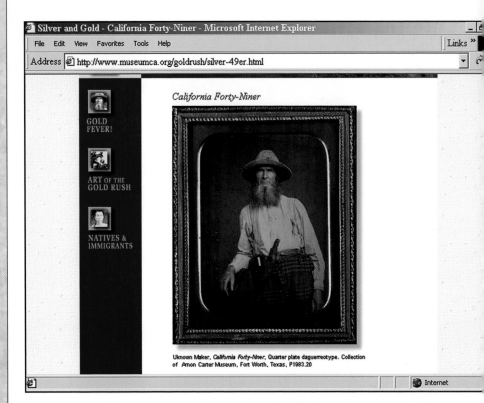

Silver and Gold - California Forty-Niner - Microsoft Internet Explorer

File   Edit   View   Favorites   Tools   Help   Links »

Address http://www.museumca.org/goldrush/silver-49er.html

GOLD FEVER!

ART OF THE GOLD RUSH

NATIVES & IMMIGRANTS

California Forty-Niner

Uknown Maker, *California Forty-Niner*, Quarter plate daguerreotype. Collection of Amon Carter Museum, Fort Worth, Texas, P1983.20

Internet

▲ *This daguerreotype shows an unidentified forty-niner, one of the many who traveled to the Golden State in search of wealth during the California gold rush of the mid-nineteenth century.*

California farmland and take control of truck farming in the state, resentment toward Asians reared its head again. It led to the passage in 1913 of the California Alien Land Act, which forbade people who were not eligible to become U.S. citizens to own farmland in the state. After the Japanese bombed Pearl Harbor, bringing the United States into World War II, Japanese Americans who lived in California were taken from their homes and placed in internment camps, known as relocation centers.[2]

▷ The Most Populous State

Since the days of the gold rush, California's population has grown every year. The development of agriculture and modern irrigation methods made more areas of the state habitable. Even a disaster such as the 1906 San Francisco Earthquake, which leveled whole streets of buildings, did not keep people from coming to California. At the beginning of the twentieth century, people moved to southern California for its citrus-fruit industry and rich oil fields. Then the Hollywood film industry emerged. Manufacturing and industry grew across the state during World War I (1914–18). Displaced farm workers from the dust-bowl region entered California during the Great Depression of the 1930s in hopes of finding work and food, and their numbers affected the state's already-slowed economy. America's participation in World War II spurred California's economy forward with the construction of ships, airplanes, and weapons.

The postwar 1950s in California were marked by the rapid rise of suburbs. And with the newly popular medium of television, Hollywood began to build new studios to film television programs. The counterculture of the 1960s pulsated in California with events such as the "summer of love," in 1967, in which 100,000 hippies gathered in San Francisco to promote peace.

California remains the fastest-growing state in the nation. Californians face serious issues with crime, air and water pollution, illegal immigration, and public health services. But the state's problems pale in comparison to all the riches that California has to offer and the spirit of Californians themselves.

Chapter Notes

Chapter 1. The State of California

1. The United States Census Bureau, "California Quick Facts," n.d., <http://quickfacts.census.gov/qfd/states/06000.html> (October 16, 2002).

2. Borgna Brunner, ed., *Time Almanac 2002* (Boston: Information Please, 2001), p. 143.

Chapter 2. Land and Climate

1. Borgna Brunner, ed., *Time Almanac 2002* (Boston: Information Please, 2001), p. 608.

2. William A. McGeveran Jr., ed., *The World Almanac and Book of Facts* (New York: World Almanac Education Group, Inc., 2002), p. 171.

Chapter 3. Economy

1. California Farm Bureau Federation, "The Century of California Agriculture," n.d., <http://www.cfbf.com/info/century.htm> (January 9, 2003).

Chapter 4. Government

1. California Historical Society, *California History Online*, "Statehood," n.d., <http://www.californiahistory.net/goldFrame-statehood.htm> (January 28, 2003).

Chapter 5. History

1. California Historical Society, *California History Online*, "Missions," n.d., <http://www.californiahistory.net/span_frame_missions.htm> (January 28, 2003).

2. Learn California.org, *A Concise Narrative of California History*, n.d., <http://www.learncalifornia.org/doc.asp?id=356> (January 28, 2003).

Further Reading

Green, Carl R. *The Mission Trails in American History.* Berkeley Heights, N.J.: Enslow Publishers, Inc., 2001.

Heinrichs, Ann. *California.* Chicago: Children's Press, 1998.

Ingram, Scott. *California: The Golden State.* Milwaukee: Gareth Stevens, Inc., 2002.

Issacs, Sally Senzell. *Life in a California Mission.* Chicago: Heinemann Library, 2002.

Kavanaugh, James. *California Trees and Wildflowers.* Whitefish, Mont.: Waterford Press, Ltd., 2000.

Kennedy, Teresa. *California.* Danbury, Conn.: Children's Press, 2001.

Motoyoshi, Michelle. *Filipinos in California.* Fremont, Calif.: Toucan Valley Publications, Inc., 1999.

———. *Mexicans in California.* Fremont, Calif.: Toucan Valley Publications, Inc., 1999.

Parker, Adam D. *People of the California Gold Rush.* Fremont, Calif.: Toucan Valley Publications, Inc., 1999.

Parker, Janice. *A Guide to California.* Calgary, Alta.: Weigl Publishers, Inc., 2000.